INDIAN
MUSIC
MAKERS

GRAY-WOLF.

INDIAN
MUSIC
MAKERS

written and illustrated by
ROBERT HOFSINDE
(Gray-Wolf)

William Morrow and Company   New York 1967

J
970.6
Hofsinde

BY THE SAME AUTHOR

THE INDIAN AND HIS HORSE

THE INDIAN AND THE BUFFALO

INDIAN BEADWORK

INDIAN FISHING AND CAMPING

INDIAN GAMES AND CRAFTS

INDIAN HUNTING

THE INDIAN MEDICINE MAN

INDIAN PICTURE WRITING

INDIAN SIGN LANGUAGE

INDIAN WARRIORS AND THEIR WEAPONS

INDIANS AT HOME

THE INDIAN'S SECRET WORLD

5 6 7 8 9   77 76 75 74

Published simultaneously in Canada by
George J. McLeod Limited, Toronto.
Printed in the United States of America.
Library of Congress Catalog Card Number 67-15149

The author acknowledges with thanks the courtesy of the Smithsonian Institution, Bureau of American Ethnology, for permission to reprint music published in the Institution's Bulletin No. 53 (1913), entitled *Chippewa Music II*, by Francis Densmore.

NOTE

The examples of Indian music in this book come from the Ojibwa, also known as the Chippewa, of northern Minnesota.

17983

CONTENTS

·|·|·|

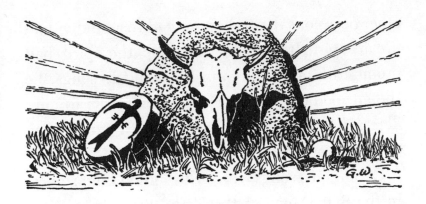

1

.|.|.| **INDIAN MUSIC**

To the American Indian, singing was a serious matter. It was a part of his whole being, from birth until the last moments of his life.

Many of his songs were prayers. Some of them were directed to the Great Spirit, the Manitou, the Orenda, or whatever the Maker of All was called by the various tribes throughout the country. On other occasions the Indian prayed to an individual dream spirit, to ask for the help the spirit had promised him in a dream. In medicine songs the Indian medicine man asked other spirits to cure illnesses, bring rain, or locate needed game when the tribe was without food.

Ceremonial songs were also of great importance. In the Sun Dance of the Teton Sioux more than forty songs were sung. Hunting songs were common among all tribes, and so were war songs. Each warrior society had its own songs, used only by its members. Certain of these songs, which the Indian believed had magical powers, had to be sung correctly in every way, or the powers would be lost.

A mother sang lullabies to her child in the cradleboard. There were songs related to children's games, and in many tribes songs to be sung before a man-child went out to seek his first vision. On his return, the Indians sang still other songs.

When a man came home from a visit with another tribe, one of the first questions he was asked was what new song he had learned. When such a song was sung, the Indians always announced from what tribe it had come.

Brave men were praised in special honoring songs. There were victory songs, too, as well as planting songs and harvest songs, canoe songs, love songs, and songs for giving and accepting gifts. And, when the Indian's time had come to take the long trail to the eternal Sand Hills, he sang a death song.

As musical accompaniment, the Indians used drums, tom-toms, and rattles. The one melody-producing instrument they had was the flute, which a young man played when he was courting a maiden. Therefore, during a ceremony the voices of the singers carried the melody, while the drums and rattles supplied the rhythm.

2

.|.|.| **TOM-TOMS**

THE skin-covered instruments upon which the Indians beat out their rhythms were commonly called drums. Many Indians, however, made a distinction between two types. A *drum* had two heads, one on each end of the cylinder or hoop, while the single-headed instrument was called a *tom-tom*.

The earliest known drumming was performed on a large, untanned animal hide. Each grasping a corner, the four drummers pulled the hide as tight as they could, and with their free hand beat upon it with slender sticks.

In time this drum was followed by a steadier type. The Indians set a number of pegs into the earth in a large circle. Over them they spread an untanned hide, holding it firmly in place by placing a hoop, made from pliable branches, on top of the

hide and slipping it down around the pegs. The drummers sat around this low drum to play.

We cannot be sure if the Indians at that time had any special traditions connected with the making of these instruments, but later, when drums and tom-toms as we know them today were made, a great deal of ceremony was involved. Before they obtained a hide, the Indians sang deer-hunting songs. While they were preparing the skins they sang other songs, and during the cutting of the hide more special songs were sung. There were songs connected with making the drum frame and, finally, songs to be sung over the finished instrument to give it power. Many of these songs were secret, known only to the individual drum maker.

When he made a tom-tom, the Indian used ash, cedar, or hickory for the frame. With his stone or bone tool he split away a long strip of wood about two inches wide. In order to make a tom-tom just over a foot in diameter, the wood strip had to be four feet long. Using a sharp flint and a piece of sandstone, the Indian worked the wood until it was smooth and measured about one fourth of an inch thick.

The wood was next soaked in water for several days to make it pliable. Then the Indian bent it into a hoop, whose ends overlapped, and drilled four holes through the overlap. At that point he lashed the frame together with a wet rawhide thong.

The head for the tom-tom was made from a piece of untanned deer hide. It, too, was soaked in water until the Indian could scrape all the hair off with a bone scraper. After he had done so, he continued to scrape the hide until it was uniformly quite thin.

When the skin was ready, the Indian spread it out and placed the frame on top of it. With a charred branch he drew a circle onto the skin, two inches larger than the frame. Along that line he cut the hide so that it was now a round drumhead. He cut a lacing thong from a leftover piece of the hide, and then he returned the skin and the thong to the water for more soaking.

While they soaked, the Indian rubbed down the sharp edges of the hoop frame with a piece of sandstone, so the frame would not cut through the head once it was in place. This step completed, he drilled a row of holes half an inch up from the lower edge of the frame. They were spaced one inch apart.

When the wet hide was soft and pliable, the Indian placed it over the frame, with its outside edge hanging down. He made a knot at one end of the lacing thong, and starting from the inner side of the frame he passed the thong in and out of the holes along the frame's lower rim, making corresponding holes through the skin. This sewing lashed the skin to the frame. Then the Indian left the tom-tom to dry in the open air or in the warmth of the lodge.

He added a grip, or handhold, underneath the head, when the tom-tom was dry. In the frame he

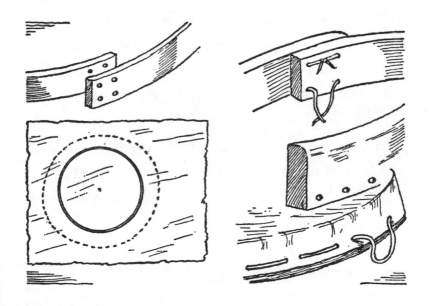

made four pairs of holes, opposite each other, so as to divide the frame into four equal parts. The paired holes were about half an inch apart. Through two sets of holes across from each other he passed a thong and knotted it. Then he passed a second thong through the remaining sets of holes, drew the ends of the thongs up tight, and knotted them.

In some tribes the Indians made the head and the handgrip all in one piece. This method called for a larger hide, because the Indian cut four long strips extending from the circular drumhead. After the hide was laced onto the frame, the extensions were merely folded under and knotted together into a handhold while they were still wet. Once dry, the knot would not come open.

The Tlingit and the Haida Indians of the Northwest Coast painted decorations on the inside of the tom-tom head. In this way they prevented the constant beating of the drumstick from wearing off the design.

Tom-tom drumsticks were usually of two types—straight and looped. The straight kind had a small groove cut near one end, and that end was covered with a wrapping of soft buckskin. The Indian tied a fine bucksin thong around the wrapping at the groove, to hold the padding.

The looped beater took a little more work. It was made from a strip of ash or hickory, eighteen inches long. At one end the Indian cut away a twelve-inch sliver, which tapered toward the middle of the stick. Then he soaked the remaining portion of this section of the drumstick in boiling water until it was pliable enough to bend into a loop, which he held in place with a wrapping of wet sinew, or a thin strip of rawhide.

Tom-toms were made and used by a number of tribes, and nearly every Indian owned one. Within the shelter and privacy of his own lodge the Indian took up his tom-tom while singing his dream songs or other personal songs.

Tom-toms were also used, with singing, to ac-

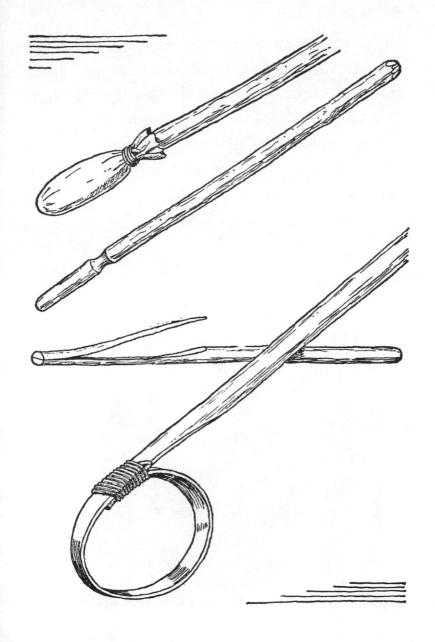

company a group of dancers. At such times there were usually four tom-toms. The drummers liked to use instruments of much the same pitch, or, as they said, "four tom-toms that sing together."

The herald, or village crier, beat on his tom-tom while riding through the camp, to call attention to his announcements.

GRAY·WOLF.

3

.|.|.| **DRUMS**

Drums, which had two heads, varied in size and diameter. The Plains Indians built them with frames from three to four inches deep, and drumheads from fourteen to sixteen inches in diameter. The frames were made in the same manner as tom-tom frames, but they were thicker, usually at least three quarters of an inch thick.

Because drums had two heads, there was no underside, and a handgrip could not be made with crosspieces. Instead, the Indian fastened a handle to the frame before he laced the heads into place. He made two holes in the frame, midway between the upper and lower rims, so the handgrip would give the drum balance when it was held. Through these holes he passed a rawhide thong, knotting it on the inner side of the frame and leaving enough of a loop for the hand to slip through. The Indian often wrapped these hand loops with buckskin or cloth.

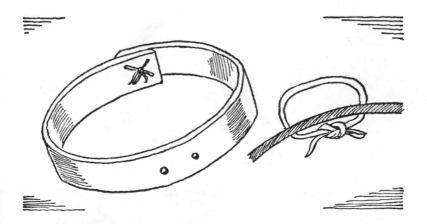

The drumheads, too, were made the same way as those used for tom-toms, and they were also measured by placing the frame on top of the skin. However, the circles for the drumheads were cut only an inch and a half larger than the frame's circumference, instead of two inches. After the Indian had trimmed the first drumhead, he drew a row of shallow scallops along its outer rim. He cut out these arches, and then he used that drumhead as a pattern for the second one. Into the points

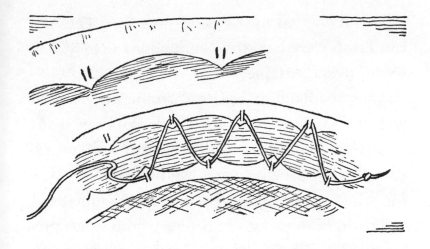

formed by the scallops, he made sets of slits, half an inch apart and half an inch long.

When both skins had been well soaked, the Indian placed them over the drum frame in such a manner that the scallops on one drumhead pointed toward the center of the arches of the other. Then he took a wet lacing thong and tied a knot in it about six inches from the end. He passed the thong through the slits in the drumheads, zigzagging from point to point. After the lacing was completed, the Indian gradually pulled the thong tight and knotted the two ends together. Thus the two heads were held together and made to fit uniformly over the frame.

The woodland tribes built some drums that were as much as eight inches deep. They made them in the same way as the shallower drums, except that the lacing thongs were longer, to allow for the greater distance between the drumheads.

These tribes also made drums whose heads produced two different tones. For one of the heads the Indians simply used a thicker skin, which made a deeper sound.

Sometimes the woodland tribes used a section of a small, hollowed-out log as a drum frame. They chose a log that was sound on the outside, but with a partially rotted inner core. They then chipped away the inside section until only a thin shell, which became the frame, remained.

The Pueblo Indians of the Southwest still use this kind of drum. However, theirs are much larger. They often measure three feet deep with

.|.|.|

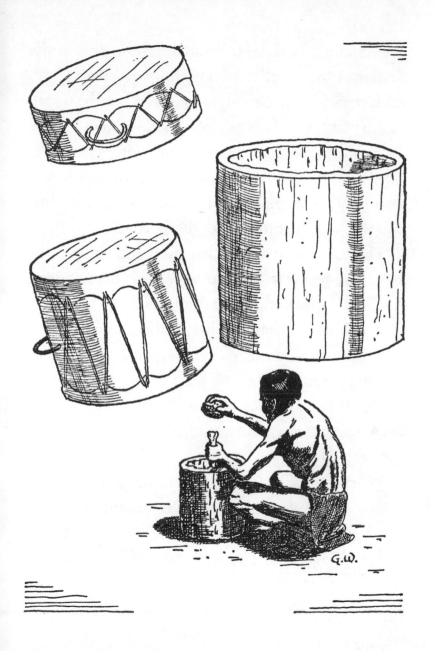

a diameter of two feet. To make these drums, the Indians trim a section of a cottonwood log at both ends to produce a barrel shape. They cut the drumheads with a scallop as deep as three inches. For lacing, they cut one slit into each long point. Before he puts the heads on, the drum maker ties two handles in place on the same side, one near the top and the other near the bottom.

The Indians employ two methods to lace the wet drumheads to the frame. When following the first, they place the points of the two heads directly above each other. This position makes the lacing form a design, for every other line of lacing thong is vertical, and the alternating line is at an angle. When following the other method, the Indians stagger the points, and the lacing forms even, elongated triangles.

To the finished drum the Indians add colors, which give a pleasing effect. They stain the drumheads black, and they paint the spaces between the scallops white. The long, triangular spaces be-

tween the lacing thong they fill in with alternating red and blue.

This type of drum is quite heavy. When it is in use, at a dance, for example, the drummer hangs it by one loop from a trimmed-down projecting limb on a stout, straight sapling. In this way he can support it easily.

The Chippewa and the Menominee, who lived in the Great Lakes region, also made large drums, but not until after they came into contact with white men. Early in 1659, the French explorer Pierre Radisson and his men were at Lake Superior. Later in that century more and more French came and settled in the beautiful north

country we now call Minnesota. Among the items they brought with them, and later built, were big wooden washtubs. The Indians obtained some of these tubs, and before long they began converting them into frames for ceremonial drums.

The solid bottom of a tub would have deadened the sound of the drum, so the Indians cut a large round section out of the bottom. The skins for the drumheads were scraped, cut, soaked, and then laced to the frame, with a great deal of ceremony and singing each step of the way. Because a washtub tapers downward, the upper drumhead was larger than the lower one.

At equal distances below the top rim the Indians drilled four sets of holes. They tied loops through the holes with which to carry and to hang the drum. Two inches below the upper rim they made two more holes, one opposite the other, through which they stretched a rawhide thong. They tied a metal sleigh bell to the middle of the thong. Beating upon the drumhead produced vi-

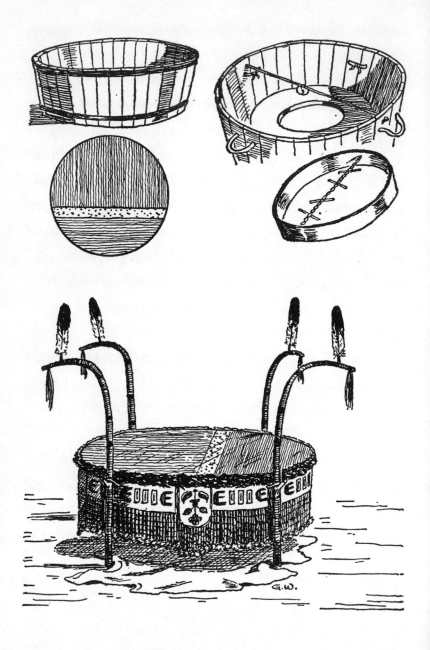

brations that jangled the bell, adding its ring to the sound of the drum.

On some of the smaller hand drums four short, narrow pieces of wood were inserted into a thin, double-twisted strand of sinew. This device made a rattle, which served the same purpose as the bell.

Lacing was done with the zigzag method, but the Indians later covered it with a broad strip of trade cloth, or flannel, which was usually bright red. The upper half of the band was further covered with a wide band of beadwork, and below the red cloth was a narrower band of dark blue.

Around the topmost rim of the drum the Indians fastened a two-inch-wide strip of otter fur, and the lower part of the drum was covered with long beaded fringes in several colors. The drumhead itself was painted in blue, yellow, and red.

These large hanging drums were very special. There were two kinds, chiefs' drums and warriors' drums. Of the two, the warrior's drum was a little smaller. Sometimes, too, they were called friendship drums or presentation drums. The drums had these names because a chief could present one to a chief of another tribe, or a warrior might make a presentation of one to another warrior, even within his own tribe. These affairs always called for a great deal of ceremony—singing and dancing and, of course, a large feast.

When it was in use, the drum was suspended slightly above the ground from four curved stakes, or, as the Indians called them, the four legs. These legs were set firmly into the ground, and the above-ground sections were fully covered with beadwork. The young saplings used for the legs were carefully selected for uniformity in size and proper placement of their branches. The Indians trimmed a peg from a branch at the same height on each sapling, and from these pegs they were able to hang the drum evenly. After the Indians trimmed and peeled the four saplings, they bent the upper ends and fastened them down to the ground, forming four equal arches.

.|.|.|

The upper ends of the legs curved away from the drum, and the top of each arch was decorated with an eagle feather and tufts of horsehair. Two of the arches represented north and west, and their horsehair was dyed blue. Those pointing east and south had red-dyed horsehair. On the chief's drum the eagle feathers were set in sockets to make them stand erect. On the warrior's drum the eagle feathers hung suspended from the arches.

The leading drummers used four decorated drumsticks. The beating ends were wrapped in soft buckskin, and at the base of the wrapping was a band of otter fur.

There was also a larger drumstick, which was used only by the owner, or custodian, of the drum for special rituals. This drumstick was over three feet long and was curved slightly at one end. That end was covered with the skin from the neck of a loon, its glossy feathers dotted with white.

From eight to ten ordinary drumsticks were kept on hand for use by the relief drummers.

Two pipes belonged with the drum as well. One, which had a flat stem, was smoked only by the drum owner and the four principal drummers. The second had a longer, rounded stem. It was called a warrior pipe, and it could be smoked by the relief drummers or by anyone to whom it was offered.

Lastly, two wooden containers, or boxes, were kept with the drum. One was made to hold the eagle feathers when the drum was not in use. The

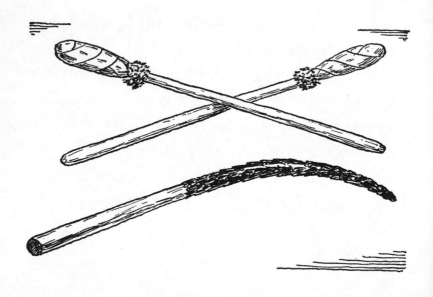

other was divided in the middle, with one compartment to hold tobacco, and the other to hold the red willow bark that was mixed with the tobacco. In later years the box was made with three compartments, and the center one held ordinary kitchen matches for lighting the pipes.

The Cree Indians in Canada made a rather unusual drum. It was square, and its wood frame was pegged together at the corners. Each side was be-

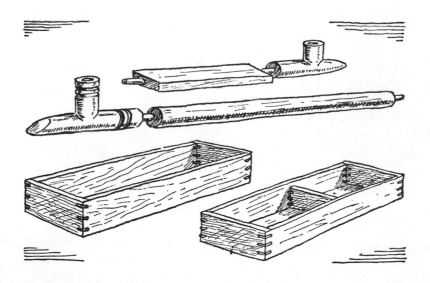

tween sixteen and eighteen inches long, and the handle was placed at the center of one side.

The Northwest Coast Indians used wooden boxes for drums. In some villages the box drum was made from cedar, and it was large enough and long enough so that several men could sit on its top. They beat out the rhythm for the dances by banging their heels against the side of the box.

In other villages along the coast Indians made long, narrow boxes, which they suspended from the rafters inside their plank houses so that the drums hung waist high. The drummers lined up alongside them and beat out the tempo with their fists. So that they would not hurt their hands they wrapped them in soft, shredded cedar bark.

The Ojibwa, the Iroquois, and to some extent the Navaho used another type of drum—the water drum. In the performance of the Ojibwa's Grand Medicine Ceremony it was the principal instrument, and they called it a Mide drum. They made it from a hollowed-out log, usually basswood, and

it was about sixteen inches tall. Its frame was tapered slightly, giving it a diameter of approximately ten inches at the bottom and eight and a half inches at the top.

The drumhead was made from an untanned deerskin, which the Indian held in place by slipping a circular wood rim over it and the frame. Into the side of the frame the drum maker drilled a hole, and through it he poured water into the drum. When it was partly filled, he closed the hole with a wooden plug. The splashing water within the drum against the drumhead created the proper tone. The tone could be changed by varying the amount of water inside the drum.

The Ojibwa painted a blue band all around the base of the Mide drum, and they decorated the drum itself with four figures, which represented four spirits, outlined in red. An oblong figure, painted blue, stood for a bag of yarrow. Yarrow is an herb that was once used as a tonic and as a cure for colds. To the Ojibwa it was a symbol for life.

The Iroquois water drum, which was also made from basswood, was slightly smaller. It measured from six to twelve inches in diameter, but its frame was only seven inches high. The Iroquois hollowed out a section of a log all the way through and fitted a wooden bottom tightly to the lower end. They held it in place with a coating of spruce gum, which also made it waterproof. They filled their drum

about one third full of water. Like the Ojibwa Mide drum, the tone quality could be changed by varying the level of water.

The drumsticks of the Iroquois were small, but they often carved them with beautiful designs.

The Navaho's water drum worked on the same principle. However, it was made from a clay water jar. A piece of buckskin was stretched over its mouth and held in place by a buckskin thong.

4

.|.|.|

RATTLES

DANCE and medicine rattles varied in size, shape, and materials according to their tribal origin. Buffalo horn, bark, rawhide, wood, and gourds were used, as well as such assorted articles as whole turtles, turtle shells, hoofs, and the dewclaws of the deer. The Indians in various parts of the country employed the natural materials available in their own region to make their rattles.

.|.|.|

Among the buffalo hunting tribes, the horns of that shaggy animal were found to be good rattle material. The Indians cut a section of horn to the desired size and scraped away its insides until only a thin shell remained. Then they fitted a thick piece of rawhide into the open top and bottom of the horn, holding it in place with glue made from horn scrapings boiled in a little water. In the center of the end pieces the Indians made holes and dropped in a few pebbles. Then they added a wood handle. The uppermost tip of the handle protruded slightly through the top part of the rattle. This tip and the handle itself were wrapped with a few turns of wet sinew to keep the handle from slipping.

After knives with steel blades were obtainable, the Indians often whittled handles with a thinner section that fitted inside the rattle. In later years, too, thin wood discs took the place of the rawhide end pieces, and in some cases they were held in place with brass upholstery nails.

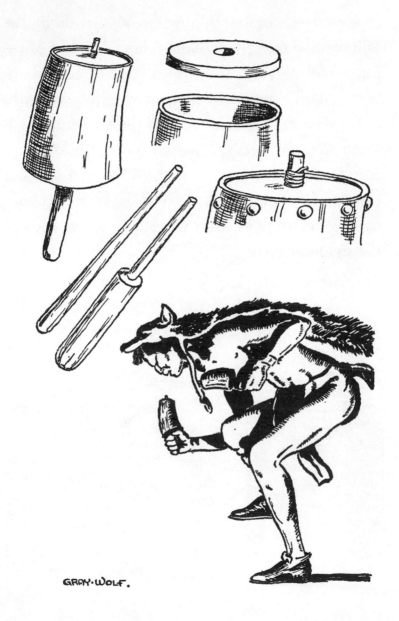

GRAY·WOLF.

A rattle of comparable design was made by the Ojibwa and other woodland tribes. Instead of using a buffalo horn, they cut a strip of birch bark and soaked it in hot water so it would bend without cracking. Then they shaped the bark into a cylinder and stitched it together along the overlap, using strands of spruce root. With two circular pieces of wood, which were held in place with small wooden pegs, they closed the open ends of the cylinder.

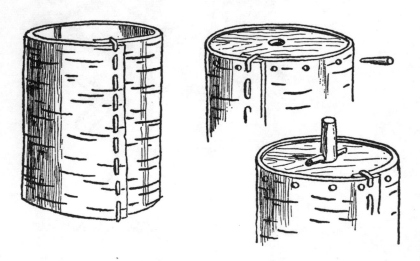

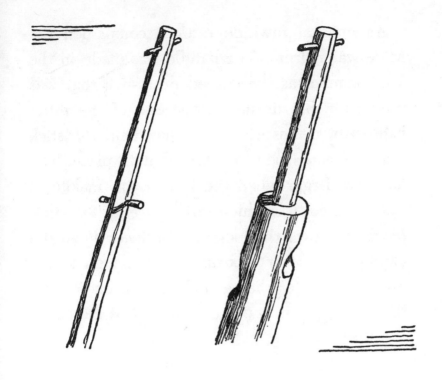

Some rattles were secured to the handle by a peg which was inserted through the handle, flush with the top and bottom piece of wood. Other handles were made with a carved handgrip, which held the rattle in place.

An unusual rawhide rattle accompanied the Mide water drum. The handle was made in the same manner as the curved drumstick that was used with that drum. At one end of the rattle handle—or drumstick—the Indian bent the stick into a circular loop and lashed it in place. The loop was larger when the Indian was making a rattle. He cut a rawhide rattle cover with a tail-piece to fit over the loop and partway down the handle. The cover was made big enough to lap over itself. After the rawhide had been soaked, the Indian put it in place and stitched the edges together.

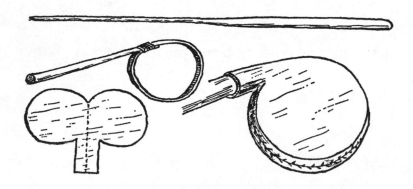

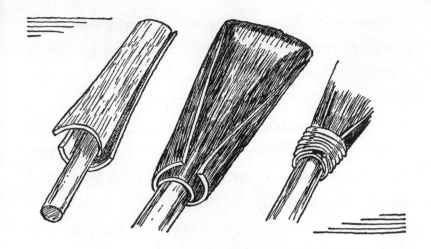

One of the simplest rattles was made by the Iroquois. Selecting a twelve-inch-long elm branch, the Indian slit the bark carefully along two sides from end to end. He removed the two bark strips and discarded one of them. Then he scored the remaining strip across the center, folded it back on itself, and brought the sides together, so that it made a container. Into the container he dropped a few pebbles; then he inserted one end of the branch into it, tying the bark to the branch with a wrapping of wet sinew or rawhide. The branch formed the rattle handle, and the bark was the rattle itself.

The Plains Indians made a very interesting rattle from rawhide. It was often used by medicine men or, when decorated with fur, by some of the Sioux Warrior Society members.

First the maker of the rattle cut two round pieces of rawhide, about five inches in diameter, each with a short extension that would fit around the rattle handle. He soaked them in water until they became very soft, and then he stitched them together along the edges in much the way a base-

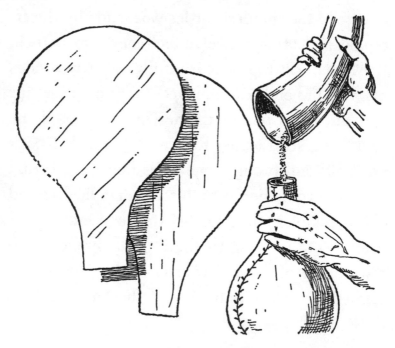

ball is sewed. Through the neck opening of this rounded pouch the Indian then poured wet sand. As he poured he poked the sand down solidly with a stick, at the same time working and forming the rawhide into a rounded shape. Then he set the filled skin aside to dry.

When the sand was completely dry, the Indian poured it out and fitted a wooden handle firmly into the neck opening, holding it in place with the usual wrapping of wet sinew.

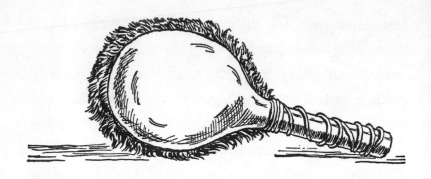

Members of the Strong Hearts Warrior Society of the Teton Sioux covered the sewing on their rattles with an inch-wide band of beaver, otter, or muskrat fur, which extended up, over, and around the rattle. The ends of the fur strip and the rattle handle itself were then partly covered with a wrapping of buckskin.

After the Indians could obtain cloth they often wrapped the handles with red or blue scraps of felt, then added the buckskin wrapping as before.

The Iroquois False Face Society used large snapping turtles in their rituals. After killing the turtles by suffocation, the Indians removed the legs from their skin and cleaned out the interior. Then they hung up the shell to dry.

Once the turtle had dried, the Iroquois soaked the leg skins, dropped some large pebbles into them, and sewed the skins together again. They next made two crosswise slits near the middle of the upper shell, and another in the center of the under shell. Into each slit they laid a long, thin sliver of cedar wood. Then they pulled the neck of the turtle to its full length. The slivers extended

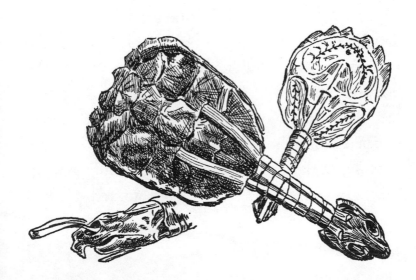

along the neck, two on the upper side, one along the underside. With strips of rawhide or buckskin, the Indians then wrapped the turtle's extended neck, which became the handle. They passed a buckskin thong through the eye sockets and knotted the ends together to form a loop for hanging up the rattle when it was not in use.

The Indians of the Southwest also made turtle rattles, but they used only the shell, and the turtles were smaller. These rattles were not held in the hand, but were fastened on the outer side of the leg, just below the knee. Through the section of the shell near the head, the Indians drilled two holes. They passed a leather tie string through the first hole, across the shell, and back through the second, knotting the ends together. Where the leather crossed the front of the shell, they tied pieces of bone, and as the wearer danced the bone struck against the hollow shell.

Most of the rattles used by the Southwestern tribes, however, were made from gourds. Gourds

grow in many shapes and sizes, but the ones that
were used in the Southwest were either large and
fully rounded, or slightly flattened on two sides.

After picking the gourds from the vine, the Indian left them to dry. During this process the meat
and the seeds inside the gourd dried up. When the
Indian made holes for the handle, he could then
readily scrape out the pulp.

The bottom hole was cut larger than the one at
the top, and the handle, which was rather short,

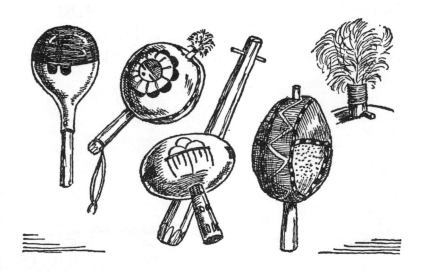

was made in the shape of a small club. When the Indian inserted it through the gourd, a twist or two usually held it securely in place. At the point where the handle protruded through the top of the gourd, he decorated it with short feathers or plumes. The gourd itself was covered with painted designs and symbols representing rain, clouds, hail, lightning, and other figures associated with the rituals and legends of the Indians of the Southwest.

Some Plains Indians used smaller gourds, but they made the handle quite long, and their decorations adorned the handle alone rather than the rattle as well. They hung tufts of horsehair, usually dyed red, from the protruding end of the handle, and they covered the full length of the long handle with fine beadwork.

Most rattles were shaken, but the Iroquois also banged theirs. Straddling a log, or a wood bench in the longhouse, the masked figure beat the edge of his turtle rattle hard against the seat.

In some of the Ojibwa rituals the rattle was shaken in a circular motion, clockwise, to indicate the direction traveled by the sun and the moon.

When he was praying for rain, the medicine man of the Navaho shook his rattle in a strong downward motion. This gesture represented the direction of falling rain, which was all-important to him in the arid country of his home. The Navaho still perform this rite today.

The most beautiful and the most elaborate Indian rattles were those made by the Northwest Coast tribes. These Indians were great carvers of totem poles, canoe prows, and house posts. It is little wonder, therefore, that their art also extended to the making of rattles.

Their most detailed rattles had carvings representing figures from their legends and tribal mythology. They carved them from solid blocks of cedar, and after they finished the design, they split the wood in half and carefully hollowed out the two sections. The handle was carved as a part of the rattle, and they split it along with the rest.

In the hollowing-out process the Indian took much care not to cut into the edges of the two halves, as any such nicks would prevent them from fitting together properly at the finish. When the rattle was hollow, the Indian drilled holes in pairs, one on each side of the joining edges. Through them he passed a spruce root or a thin strip of hide, with which he tied the two halves together. He drilled a hole through the solid handle and hammered in a tightly fitting dowel to hold it together.

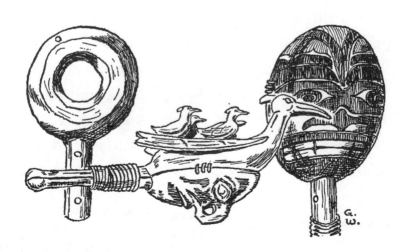

Then he painted all the carved details in red, blue, black, dull green, and white. He made the colors from earth pigments and copper, which were ground into a paint substance by mixing them with fish eggs, usually those of the salmon.

Some rattles represented faces, and others were made in a doughnut shape. However, the process of splitting, hollowing out, and joining the halves of the rattle was always the same.

There were other Indian rattles that differed from those just described in that they were not hollowed out to hold pebbles or shot.

One of them was a notched stick, which the Indians made from a long, flat piece of wood. The underside of the stick was slightly rounded, and the tip end was curved. Along the upper edge the Indians cut a row of shallow notches, and on the handle they carved the head of a bird. To use the instrument, a man placed the curved end on a small drum or on a folded piece of rawhide—anything that could serve as a sound box, or resonator. Holding the notched stick by its handle, the user rubbed a deer bone along the notches, which produced a clacking sound. These sticks were used by several tribes, including the Sioux, the Omaha, the Chippewa, the Blackfeet, and the Southwest tribes, as an accompaniment to their drumming and singing.

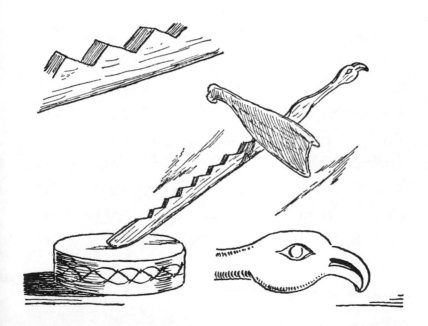

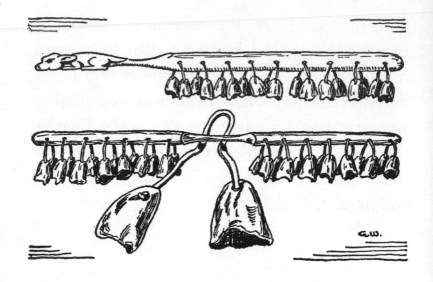

Some rattles were made from deer's dewclaws
or from slivers of deer hoofs. There were two styles
of them. One type was a flat stick with a carved
handle at one end. From the handle to the tip the
Indians drilled holes, through which they passed
buckskin thongs. They tied the dewclaws or hoof
slivers to the ends of these thongs, so that the
claws hung in pairs. This kind of rattle often had
as many as ten pairs of dewclaws along its length.

The second type of rattle was a round stick from which the dewclaws hung. A space was left free, in the center of the stick, for the handgrip.

When a man shook a dewclaw rattle, the claws clacked together. The sound produced was never as loud as that of the hollow rattles. These softer ones were employed mostly by the medicine men in their rituals.

A noisemaker was used in many tribes, along with the rattles, drums, and tom-toms. It was simply a rounded stick, about twelve inches long, which was split lengthwise down the middle for about six inches. The Indian held it in one hand and struck the split side against the open palm of his other hand, producing a clapping sound.

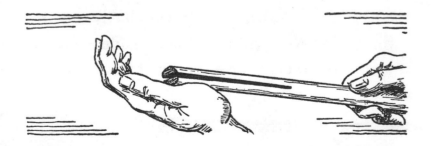

5

.|.|.| **THE COURTING FLUTE**

THE only melody-producing instrument the Indians had was the flute. To play it, a person blew into one end. He controlled the harmonic series of tones through the use of a set of finger holes along the body of the instrument. It was chiefly used by a young man who was courting a maiden, and on it he played to her a love song he had composed.

The flute had one other use, however, in time of war. If an enemy was known to be nearing the village, a man played the flute around the camp, using a melody that was understood by the people to be a warning. The enemy, hearing it, supposed it to be merely a young man playing to his sweetheart.

Straight-grained wood such as cedar or sumac was used to make the flutes, although from time to time other materials were substituted. I have a typical Winnebago flute in my collection, and it was made in the following way. First the Indian rounded off and smoothed the selected stick of wood, and then split it lengthwise into two equal parts. He next hollowed out each half until only an outer shell remained. He left a narrow, solid section, which formed a wall about six inches from the mouthpiece.

On the outside of the flute, on what might be termed the top of the instrument, the Indian cut a shallow lengthwise depression into the wood, only an eighth of an inch deep. He centered it just above the inner wall, and it was two inches long. Then he made two square holes, on either side of the wall in the depression, for air vents.

Next the Indian cut a piece of birch bark to fit into the shallow depression. This piece was three quarters of an inch wide and two inches long, and it was about as thick as a piece of cardboard. He made an opening in the center of this strip, as wide as the holes cut into the flute and as long as the distance from one to the other.

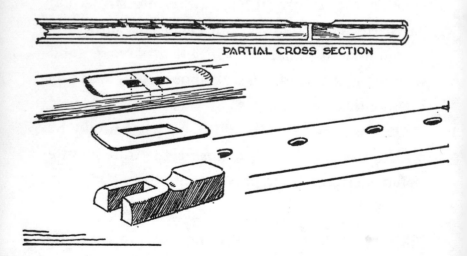

PARTIAL CROSS SECTION

The Indian then cut a small rectangular block of wood and carved two squared prongs at one end of it. He cut a curved depression into the block, placed it over the bark strip, and held it there by wrapping a thin buckskin thong around this "saddle." The prongs fitted around an air vent so the block did not cover it.

Six finger holes, each an eighth of an inch in diameter, were then drilled along the top of the flute. The Indian glued the two halves of the flute together and bound them with strips of wet sinew,

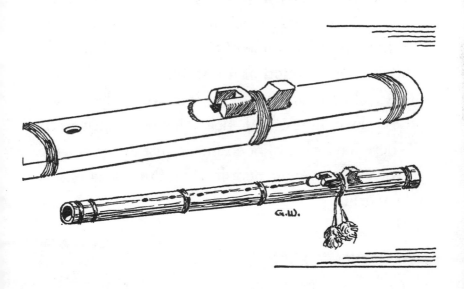

which, as it dried and pulled tight, made the flute airtight.

To test the pitch of the flute, the Indian placed the blowing end to his lips, put three fingers of each hand over the finger holes, and blew into the flute. If the tone was too high or too low, he slid the block forward or back. Once he had arrived at a clear, mellow tone, he often set the block in a permanent position with the aid of a little glue or melted pine pitch.

These courting flutes varied in size, but the usual length was that of the distance from the inside of a man's elbow to the tip of his middle finger.

The Zuñi Indians made flutes from pottery clay, and in later years some of the Plains Indians made flutes from a section of a gun barrel.

An old Indian, when he was asked how long these love flutes had been in use, answered: "There have always been flutes, just as there have always been young people. The flute is as old as the world."

6

INDIAN SONGS

INDIAN songs have many origins. The tribal songs that were used in the age-old rituals and ceremonies, the medicine men's songs, and the special, personal songs came to the Indians in dreams and visions.

Songs used during important ceremonies originated during times when the tribe was in great need. Perhaps the people were ill, and many of them were going to the Sand Hills, or perhaps meat no longer hung on the drying racks. In the midst of such trouble, the great men of some tribe sought a vision to bring help to their people.

When a vision did come, the seeker was usually given many instructions and told he must learn many new songs. The songs then became a part of the tribal life. A ritual using the songs was begun, and in following years it was usually celebrated at the exact time of year when it was first performed. These songs were passed on from one generation to the next, and they could only be sung by people of high standing in the tribe.

Medicine songs were those a medicine man received in his quest for help and power to cure his people. The personal songs were given to an individual warrior as he sought a vision that would help him overcome certain problems of his own. Often these problems centered on war or hunting. A man might, for example, have been wounded whenever he participated in a war expedition, or maybe he had never had the chance to count coup, that is, to strike an enemy.

Indian songs may sound a little discordant to a white man who hears them for the first time. The Indian sings certain notes not found in our scale, and he can sing a little above or below a note. Furthermore, an Indian song may begin in three-four time, only to change to two-four time, and, after a few measures, change back again to three-four. Our songs rarely if ever change beat in this way.

Another great difference between white and Indian songs is that whereas the songs of the white people tend to end on a high note, most of the Indian songs gradually descend through the last part of the melody, ending on a low note.

The drumming accompanying an Indian song can have a different rhythm from that of the melody. In some songs the drumming lags behind at the beginning. Then the drummer may catch up to the singer, follow along with him for a while, and fall behind again near the end of the song. An Indian accompanying his own singing is able to drum this way without the least trouble.

Not all Indian songs came from dreams or visions. Many told a story or were actually composed for a certain occasion. The first song a Chippewa Indian heard was a lullaby, sung to him by his mother while he was still in his cradleboard. A typical example is the song below. It is wordless; only the soft, crooning *we, we* sound, which makes the baby sleep, runs through it, and there is no tom-tom accompaniment.

we we we we we   we we we we we   we we we we

When the Chippewa child grew a little older, he heard other songs offered up for his well-being during his naming ceremony. Still the tribal songs had no meaning for him until he listened to and understood the tribal legends. In many of these tales the leading character, usually some animal known to the region, sang a song.

In the song below the two words meaning *coon* and *dead* are the only words used. In the tale, however, it is told that the coon is merely playing dead. In this song, as in others, only two or three words are used. The rest of the melody is sung with meaningless syllables, such as *we, he, o* or *e, a, wa, he.*

E - si-bun ni-bo

Esibun ....Coon
Nibo ....Dead

There were three general types of individual songs: songs received in dreams, songs purchased from their owner, and songs praising a man's success or generosity. The first two kinds were believed to have magic power, while the others were regarded as an honor and their singing was usually rewarded with gifts.

The first song received by a Chippewa Indian in a dream was a boy's "vision song." Among most tribes a boy, at the age of about twelve years, customarily blackened his face and then went to some secluded place to fast for several days. There he sought a dream, or vision, in which he would see his personal spirit helper, who would give him a song. In later years, whenever he needed help, the Indian sang this song and performed certain prescribed acts.

Before a Chippewa boy left on this vigil, his grandfather, or an uncle, sang the following song to him. In it the *nest* referred to is the resting place the boy will make for himself.

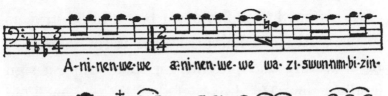

A-ni-nen-we-we a-ni-nen-we-we wa-zi-swun-nim-bi-zin-

da-go-ne

Aninenwewe ....The receding sound
Waziswun ....of the nest
Nimbizindagone ......I listen to it

Upon the boy's return, his grandfather again sang to him, this time giving him water to drink since the boy had not been permitted any during his fast all through the vigil.

In time, the boy was called upon to help with the hunting, which supplied the family with meat. Sometimes he might be successful, or sometimes he might fail, going out again and again, only to return empty-handed.

In his need the Chippewa boy offered prayers to his vigil spirit helper, asking it for guidance. After fasting and praying for some time, a sign finally came. He dreamed that he was walking near a hill, and from beyond it he heard voices. Climbing the hill, he saw a herd of deer standing in a circle. The leader of the deer said it was time to dance as they always did when the leaves were off the trees. He then pointed to a small buck whose horns had grown higher than his ears, saying he should be the one to sing. The young buck sang this song:

Ki-

we-wi-na-ko-wi-nĕ   be-jig ai-ya-bĕ

Kiwewinakowine ...... Straight-horned

Bejig .... One
Aiyabe .... Buck

Thus the Chippewa boy learned the song, and it became his hunting song, bringing him success on the hunting trail.

As his skill grew someone might want to buy his song. He could ask a lot for this favor. Two or three horses were considered a fair price. The sale of a song was actually an agreement by the owner to share the song with another man, since the owner continued to use the song as he had in the past. In this manner songs were perpetuated over the years.

Once the young Chippewa had become a hunter, it was only a question of time before he joined a group on the war trail. These war parties were mostly directed at the Sioux, who then lived in Minnesota, and whom the Chippewa finally drove across the Mississippi River.

Whenever a war party was reported to be on

the way home, some of the villagers went out to meet them. As soon as they heard what had happened, they hurried back to the village to spread the news. If a man had been exceptional in his deeds, upon entering the camp he would be greeted with the following Honor Song, sung by some of the old women.

O-ki-tci-ta mi-gĭ-sĭns

Okitcita .... Leader of the warriors
Migisins .... (is) Little Eagle

Still another type of song was used to honor a great brave. In the long-ago days, a great Chippewa warrior once had been honored with a special song, and his valor had never been forgotten. Ever since this song has been used to honor a new and brave man, the only change being the substitution of the new brave's name for that of the old brave. Such an honor was usually bestowed upon the warrior through the medicine man who had been on the war trail with the party. When the song ended, the honored man always gave the singer a gift.

Again the song has only two translatable words, the rest of the sounds being meaningless syllables. The reason is that the deeds of the warrior for whom the song was originally made up were so well known to the Chippewa people, that it was thought needless to mention them.

Although the new brave is called *ogima*, or chief, the use of that term does not mean he is a chief or that he is about to become one. It simply means that he conducted himself in a manner becoming a great leader.

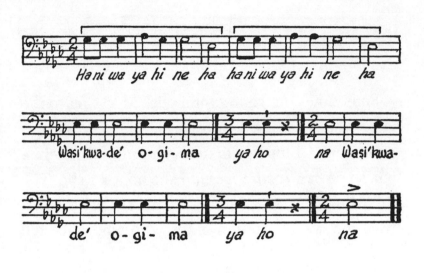

Hani wa ya hi ne ha hani wa ya hi ne ha

Wasi'kwa-de' o-gi-ma ya ho na Wasi'kwa-

de' o-gi-ma ya ho na

Wasikwade .... The warrior's name
Ogima .... Chief

Once a young Chippewa man proved himself as a warrior and a good hunter, it was time for him to think about a wife and a lodge of his own. Usually there was one girl in the village to whom he was attracted, and he began to court her with his flute, playing a melody much like the one below.

Sometimes the young man wished to sing to the girl and did not use a flute at all.

A young Chippewa maiden also sang to the man whose *sit-beside-him-woman* she hoped to be. The following song was sung by a young girl the first time she saw the Indian brave with whom she fell in love.

Nia	Oh
Nindinendum	I am thinking
Mekawianin	I have found
Ninimucen	my lover

The courting continued for some time, but at last a member of the young man's family went to the parents of the girl and made the proper arrangements. When the day was set for the ceremony, the girl's family prepared for the feast, inviting friends and relatives, making new costumes, and erecting a wigwam for the newlyweds to move into.

After the wedding ceremony and feast, the young couple gave thanks to those who had brought gifts. The song of "thanks for a gift" differs from the other songs in that the words are not sung, but are spoken between performances of the song, which is repeated several times. The drum is struck only once in a measure and always follows the voice.

Tciwawicendum ......I am very grateful
Endodawid ....For what he is doing for me

Singing was not relegated to the Chippewa men alone, for although they had their important war and hunting songs, their social and ceremonial songs, the women had their songs too. The lullaby and the woman's love song are two examples, but there were still other songs of equal importance.

Among the Chippewa, the making of maple sugar was a pleasant industry. When spring arrived in the North, the people came from their scattered winter camps and assembled in the maple groves to tap the trees of their flowing sap.

During the tapping, the boiling, and the general preparation for sugar making, the events of the past winter were fully discussed and general sociability marked the gathering.

Since everyone wanted an abundant supply of this favorite luxury, the women sang this song, which is very old, to make the sap flow freely. It is so old, in fact, that the words are today obsolete in the Chippewa language.

And so, as he grew older, the Chippewa Indian learned more and more songs. The man or woman who became a member of the Grand Medicine Society, the Midewiwin, had to be able to sing many songs belonging to this native religion of the tribe. The society had eight degrees, but as the initiation into each was costly, most mem-

Wi·dji·ga·wi·ni - na·ha hin·di·yan - e wi·dji·ga·wi·ni -

na·ha hin·di·yan - e wi·dji·ga·wi·ni - na·ha hin·di·yan-

e wi·dji·ga·wi·ni - na·ha hin·di·yan - e wi·dji·ga·wi·ni -

na·ha hin·di·yan - e mi·ti·ga·wi·ni - na·ha hin·di·yan-

e gi·gi·gog wi·ni - na·ha hin·di·yan - e wi·dji·ga·wi·ni -

na·ha hin·di·yan - e wi·dji·ga·wi·ni - na·ha hin·di·yan-e

Mitigon'.................................. From the trees
Gion'gigog' The sap is freely flowing

bers reached only the fourth degree. Those who passed through them all in time mastered several hundred songs, which were an important part of the long rituals.

For the ceremony in which a chief or a warrior presented a drum to another chief or warrior, more songs had to be learned. Among them were the Song of the Chief and the Song of the Speaker. They were followed by the Song of the Owner of the Drum, Song of the Warriors, and the Song of Giving Away the Drum. The entire ceremony lasted nine days, and if there were any members of the tribe who were in mourning and had been for at least six months, they were invited to the dancing on the first day. At that time a song was sung for them called the Song of Restoring the Mourners. Their faces were painted, and if they were women, the part in their hair was painted red. Then a song called the Song of Painting the Faces was sung.

Divorces sometimes took place among the Chippewa Indians, and this ceremony involved four songs. It was usually held on the last day of dancing during the drum ceremony, and in the early days it is said to have been quite simple. The man or woman desiring the divorce went through the motion of throwing something outside the dance circle during the singing of the Divorce Songs.

Twelve more songs in all belonged to the actual drum ceremony.

Aside from these songs, the Chippewa also had Planting and Harvesting Songs, the Moccasin Game Songs, and songs for entertaining the small children. Many of their songs were directed to things in nature: to animals and birds, the sky, water, clouds; to thunder and the thunderbird; and to the four winds.

In the old days an Indian's entire life centered upon this form of expression, and there were even songs surrounding the end of his life. If a man was mortally wounded in battle, then with his last breath he sang his Death Song. If the Messenger from the Spirit World came to him in his old age, then within the darkness of his own lodge he took up his drum or tom-tom and in a strong voice sang the Death Song. Once his soul had departed, his wife covered herself with her robe and keened in mourning. Thus the Indian's life began and ended in song.

7

·|·|·| **INDIAN SONGS TODAY**

IN spite of all the changes that have come to the life of the Indian, the old songs and the dances are being preserved. The war songs are sung, but today the words describe the deeds of the modern Indian soldier rather than the brave of old. Now the Indians sing of their pride in the Stars and Stripes, just as their forefathers sang to the glory of the feather-trimmed war flag of their day. The Indian mother croons the same lullaby to her baby that her own mother and grandmother used. An Indian love song is used in courting, but now and then the English words *I love you* appear.

Only among the most remote Indian villages are some of the old ceremonies still observed. There the old men, who sit by the fire to dream and talk of the days of their youth, still find meaning in the ancient songs. In the Southwest, perhaps more than any other place today, faith in prayer songs and ceremonial dances remains. At many of the rituals in that region no white person is permitted.

Most ceremonies throughout the country, however, are open to visitors. From the Cherokee in North Carolina, through Wisconsin and Minnesota and Michigan, across the land to Sioux, Cheyenne, and Blackfeet country, the visitor is welcome, and he may bring his camera.

Should you be so fortunate as to witness one or

more of these ceremonies, forget for the moment that you are in the twentieth century. Listen instead to the songs and to the drumbeats. Look at the swaying bodies and the stomping moccasined feet. Observe the ceremonial costumes. If you watch closely and listen well, you will for those few minutes be transported back through time.

The heartbeat of the drum and the glory of its past are still with us. When the medicine man sings his song for the good of the people, he sings not only for the Indians, but for all men everywhere.

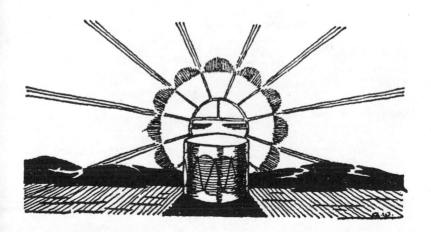